TO SET US FREE

To Set Us Free

poetry by

BETTE PETERSON

Powerful Owl Press

Copyright © 2016 by Bette Peterson

All rights reserved. No part of this book may be reproduced in any manner whatsoever without written permission except in the case of brief quotations embodied in critical articles and reviews.

First edition. November 1, 2016.
Copyright © 2016 Bette Peterson.

Second edition. May 1, 2022.
Copyright © 2016 Bette Peterson.

To my family and friends

~ 1 ~

THE BIRTHDAY

A birthday in the country, can anything compare
The warmth of family, Grans' and Aunts and Uncles everywhere
The wide veranda, big old lounges, babies young and fair
Cameras clicking, feet are kicking reaching for the yard
A little girl barely five excited full of joy
Cousins tormenting, full of heckling, damn the family's boys
Then Uncles saying 'Come our princess; sing a song for us' it's worth a sixpence'
Auntie wants to hear her favourite tune "now is the hour" or "Maggie" sounds good
It would make the day for us, we must go soon
Too quickly it's over and the dark has come
Little girls in bed, dreaming of years to come
Not knowing that it's in vain

~ 2 ~

MUM

My best friend is my mother
How often it's been said
I know it's not original
But with love I comprehend
The hours of sleep gone missing
Listening for the door
The years of work you gave for me
When fun was all I sought
My ironing left, you always did
Not maybe, but for sure
Sponge cakes and puddings, roasts and lamb
Cooked perfectly and sauced with your love
Now that I'm older I understand the sacrifices you made
To keep your family feeling good, the tiny price we paid
The way we always expect you to be there, and pray some way you can be
Forever and a day.

~ 3 ~

TARRANT

You have opened my heart
Your birth is a joy
Your life gives mine meaning
I live again
To treasure the sunshine
And laugh at the rain
Emerge back to joy
Through layers of pain
Little man you are lucky
For you will be loved
And when you are loved
You glimpse heaven above
God bless you

~ 4 ~

THE SYSTEMATIC WOMAN

Who is to blame for woman's plight?
The relentless work, the endless fights
The ring goes on and then it starts
The mental stress, the 'till death do us part'
Do we blame the system for teaching us this?
Or blame the man for his values amiss
Or blame the woman for complicity
Our own worst enemies? Maybe so
But to fit in the system it's all systems go!Who cares if our lives are all sorrow and woe?The machine is the judge of who it lets in
So suffer in silence to pay for your sin
For being born a woman

~ 5 ~

GRANDAD

Time moves along its nonchalant way
Meshed in the throes of my mind
Flashes of memory, a mist of yesterday
Old man with a cane and sightless eyes
Flood my brain, gentle and kind
A battered fiddle clutched in his hand
Old melodies fetched from another time
When skirts were long and money scarce
And dancers danced to another band
The whiteness of beard, the trembling limbs
Bring a legacy of past times to and pain
Leave him go, return to the present
Dissipate the mist and walk away
Leave him at peace

~ 6 ~

THE HEART

Do I see the sky or the channel of pain?
Will I be rich or a beggar for life?
To stand at the door and cry in the rain
Visions of gas fires viewed from the dark
My clothes but a covering for the worldly shell
This heart is long dead, merely a pump
The face can tell I have been to hell
Somewhere, someday I may see the light
But with you nowhere will I be
Our ways are split never to meet
Goodbye my love
Goodbye

~ 7 ~

THE LESSON

What has he done to my children?
Taught them a lesson from hell
His soul and his spirit exhausted
He made a decision to dwell
Deep in the heart of all misery
Down deep, so deep in the earth
Sending his message of evil
Begging my children to learn
Turn away from his values
Don't give him the power to use
    the tools of his own destruction
    Keep safe in the world that you choose

… 8 …

BRAIN PATH

As time slips by and grey hairs are found
We find our minds saying 'what's it about?'
To live a life of fear and shame
To ask oneself 'was I to blame?'
The unspoken words that never were said
Surely at times we made our own bed
Still we can't go back to change a thing
So accept what you are and respect your decisions
Whether good or bad they have gone forever
Go on with your life, create your own vision
The futures paths, with confidence tread
Look back with a sigh, what's gone is dead
Stare straight ahead with a stance so proud
Laugh at the sun, dismiss the clouds
My days of regret are gone forever
It's taken some time to realize I'm clever
This person who's me is not in my shade

I've thrown off my shell and emerged to the sun
I still care for the world and all God has made me
But now I can see my God's vision for me

~ 9 ~

A MESSAGE

An old lady sits on a step in Scotland
Her apron awry, her hair all grey
She sings a song of times of man
And further even, back to fey
Linked to me in so many ways
My sense of time and place secure
She startles me; whispers 'are you sure?'
The world today is fast and spinning
Hurtling towards, what? Perhaps oblivion
Then her song is heard so soft and sweet
Her words say 'stop! Smell the roses now'
Forget the future and live complete
All is in god's hands

THE ACCIDENT

The image in my head
Of a girl all dressed in blue
The car from out of nowhere
A blur of red and green
Then the blackness of the concrete
The pain of torn bruised flesh
Light rain on my face
The light of day unseen
The headlights blazing fiercely
Show the scene of crying men
Comforting the victim
Needing absolution for their sin

~ 11 ~

PAST LEA COUNTY

The paddocks abound with a bright yellow blaze
Blue sky overhead with patches of cloud
Echoing calls of Curlews and Parrots
Red earth all around with burrows and rabbits
The beauty of parched land sustaining the maze
Myriads of ground life teaming all over
Living and running under the clover
Try as we may we will never replace
The warmth of the places that childhood embraced
But somehow we know it still exists
Just out of reach
Out there in the mist

~ 12 ~

SHATTERED ILLUSIONS

In every way you destroyed my soul
By actions, words and sad, dad eyes
You ripped apart my paradise
I really believed our love was lasting
Yet with your words you smashed my world
Your actions left me in a dark turmoil
To long for what we shared together
And know deep down it has gone forever
Will I once again know happiness or walk alone
Till I can find the peace inside of one untied
From cares and fears and feeling tired
Longing for the gift of sleep
To shut my mind from worldly scenes
And dream whatever keeps me sane

~ 13 ~

SUMMER AND SPRING

Honey I still love you
Although we're far apart
You wear a ring from someone else
But still you own my heart
I cannot even speak to you
Afraid to fall apart
Your eyes still show me you are sad
To just hear your voice
Even though now it's not meant for me
Makes my heart a little lighter
An island in my sea of misery
One day if god is kind to us
We may love each other once again
If not I will remember
That summer and that spring
One space in time to call our own
And know we really cared
We loved and lost

To pressures of the world
But still if you should need me
In any way at all
    I will always be here
    Waiting for your call

~ 14 ~

THE IMAGE

Do I still love you? I really don't know
Is it an image that I want again?
Or only the fear of being alone
I know we are friends and always will stay
Close to each other no matter what may
But passion, desire? Only time will show
Can I relate to someone who caused the pain?
Or just shut the door and start again
Forget the hurt and what went before
Be there for comfort and nothing more
Love may still live where now there are stones
I really don't know

~ 15 ~

A CRY FROM THE HEART

Where is my God' I cry in vain?
To take this hurt, to ease my pain
A soul so dark, so full of hurt
Knowing only love can be the cure
Stop this ache and make me strong
To face a world that isn't pure
Where people seem so lost and bent
Climbing life's waves, so turbulent
Until they find they're tired and spent
And all they want is death

~ 16 ~

THE TIDE OF LIFE

The ocean rolls on with a mournful roar
With nothing in mind but to crash on the shore
At times it's calm is like a soft music score
Then with a crash from the heavens it turns to a cauldron
Churning and turning, taking all in its path
The sea then depicts nature's changeable wrath
To harness it might is like lighting a star
Impossible dreams that wander so far
Yet when trouble abounds and heartache remains
The sea is the cure for my anguish and pain

~ 17 ~

BUDGET TIME MUSINGS

The bureaucrats sit in their office and smile
At the power they hold with their mortar and tile
You do as we say if you live in our house
Don't dare to say boo! Just live like a mouse
The system won't let you question or fight
Go back to your cage, don't challenge their might
They will throw you a crumb from their table of plenty
The expect you to bow and beg for your food
Say thanks to them, give them your money to-boot
It won't matter to them that your tummy is empty
That your dreams are all gone; you just live for a day
No time now for laughter or the games you could play

But you can beat the system of heartache and pain
The smile of a child or the love of a friend
Will help in the struggle to feel human again"

~ 18 ~

THE ROTTING THREADS OF ME-CIETY

Our children look round and despise what they see
The standard of life shouting me, me and me
Our values are gone with the use of P.Cs
The focus is now so-called individuality
Where is the love for their sisters and brothers?
Where are the smiles that they save for another?
Just where in the world can a person belong?
They are told 'it is here' but they know that is wrong
Laws, rules, restrictions are part of their scene
Where is the freedom, not censured or mean?
Gone are the days of walking through fields
Gone is the sense that the world is for real
So don't tell our youth that they're stupid or dumb
And don't say that now they live just for fun
They know that their life will never be free
That total control is so easy to see

Just open a paper and see what they say
You'll know then for sure that there's no time for play
They must work all the time to keep up to the pace
No wonder they think that it's all a rat race
So instead of condemning their lives and their style
Please help them to live in a world of their time

~ 19 ~

BUDGET TIME '96

The treasurer sits in his big ivory tower
He smiles at the rich, at the poor he just glowers
To middle Australia he plays the good hero
To the cold and the hungry he rates a fat zero
Can he justify his attack on the poor?
If you asked him that he would show you the door
The worry is that the people can't see
The pain he brings to you and to me
They agree with the dollars he puts in their wallets
They won't even consider its out of our pockets
Many will sit at their tables and eat
While others without will sleep in the street
The Uni's will close to all, save a few
Who can put The Uni's will close to all, save a few
Who can put coins in the coffers and so pay the dues
The aged without assets will just waste away
But the rich will be kept in chocolates all day
The women who pay will have child care to spare

But the women without will just have to share
Do we all have to starve and wait for the sequel?
For a budget that's fair and strives to be equal
For people to protest and break through the glass
And battle to show the difference in class
To wait and to hope it might all change?
When enough people care to break down the frame

~ 20 ~

THE MARKET

It's Saturday morning, the traffic is fast
Weaving and passing, they don't want to be last
Pull into the driveway and then find a park
Just jostle and shove 'till you're merged in the farce
A little bit further and you'll make your mark
The person behind you is angry and cross
The person in front just thinks he's the boss
He stops for a minute to examine a glass
The young girl behind him giggles and smiles
The innocence shown is careless and free
The love for their youth is delightful to see
Merchants are anxious and spruiking their wares
Patrons are thronging, approaching their lairs
A man and his money is easy to part
He is told that he needs it, 'true, cross my heart'
The changing of tender is now so complete
They buy what they don't need, really? How sweet
The markets all flourish in so many places

And young children starve in too many cases
Why don't we learn?"

~ 21 ~

MEMORIES OF A GHOST

I slip through the door of a past, left ajar
I stand and examine my hopes from afar
Did I really believe that my dreams would come true?
That disillusionment would never intrude
An innocent child all dressed in blue
Waiting to meet someone like you
Ignore the ghost standing between you and me
If I fail to observe him he may let us be
My life is in limbo, I shrink from tomorrow
I will never admit the pain and the sorrow
The room is now fading, it's harder to see
I will slip back through the door and just let it be
If I don't concentrate on what I have seen
Tomorrow might still come true

~ 22 ~

COMPARISONS

What can I say to my girl child?
That life is meek and mild and that pigs fly
Or do I warn of the swirling pools
That swallow you whole after you try
To stand your ground and fight for your life
To flow with the currant in a comfort zone?
Or battle upstream to be covered in foam
To accept your place as a wife and a mother
Or strive to be equal, and cause quite a bother
Do I tell it's better to stay silent and still?
And that if she does not she will need a strong will
That to take her place in a man's domain
Is the choice she makes for sorrow and pain
That if you give in to the male demands
You ensure your place in pro-mans land

~ 23 ~

THE HOUSE ON THE CORNER

The only house still there next to all the flats
A house built with love and made with dads labour
We all sat and watched him toil without favour
Little by little it began to take shape
Till it stood in its glory, complete and so great
For us kids and our mum it was never so grand
No tent anymore, we all had a room
The years flew by, we were well fed and warm
We had fruit trees and vegies and beautiful flowers
Peaches and oranges with bountiful boughs
Many good times were had in its walls
Cricket was played on its lawn by us all
Then came the day that changes all our lives
It stood there now SOLD, all aged and forlorn
We kids now realise we all still mourn
The house built on the corner

~ 24 ~

ROMA

I sit here and ponder the years gone by
And think of the friendship of you and I
The mostly good memories of the times we have had
Bring back some pleasure and some tinged with sad
But the years we have shared have mostly been good
Our children have grown as we knew that they would
Our lives have been blessed by events in our past
Though fleeting at times, in our thoughts they will last
Over the years I have learned to embrace
The positive things, and others erase
But our friendship is one I will always cherish
And know these feeling will never perish
Though friends come and go in this life that's so fleeting
Our care for each other is one that's worth keeping
Though miles and events have kept us apart
Your wonderful smile has stayed in my heart
So when you feel down or a little bit flat
Give thanks for the friendship we may never have had

If we had not met life would be a little more grey
And a little bit harder along the way
When we come to the end of this wondrous time
Our friendship! The gift no one can deny

~ 25 ~

UNITY

We came together to learn from each other
With pain involved, and grief and sorrow
At time we cried, at times we smiled
But through it all we saw tomorrow
The hidden hurts were plain to see
A hundred times the hammer fell
Our lives it seems were lived in hell
But steel is strong and stands the heat
Our flowers survived with little care
Now they all know how to dare
They take a bow, stand tall and say
I will not live in yesterday
My future's bright and all can see
I live my life with dignity
The screams, the blood, the bruises too
Is shown to all, to set us free
No longer will we hide and shrink
Fearing what the night will bring

We know for us it will be light
We now all see WE'VE WON THE FIGHT
WE ARE THE WINNERS

~ 26 ~

TIME CAPSULE

I sit here and think of the years gone by
The fun times I've had and the times I've cried
The first recognition of family and friends
Times meant for pleasure or time to amend
My fun or favour still in the future
No time to think about the years I mature
I just live for the hours I enjoyed in my teens
Beaches and dances and parties supreme
Then I was a mother and all of that changed
Nappies and knitting, late nights all just waned
From going to bed at midnight or more
My resting times changed to about 7 to 4
Then came the kids teen years of stress and some strife
"Worrying eventually if all would come right
Now here I sit a grandmother and elder
And finally see that no matter my musings it was all meant to be.

Bette Peterson is an Australian author. She lives in Melbourne Victoria. To Set Us Free is the second edition of her first book of poetry.

www.ingramcontent.com/pod-product-compliance
Lightning Source LLC
Chambersburg PA
CBHW070739020526
44118CB00035B/1764